The Fifth Season

...the Season of the Heart
Inspired by Nature's Changing Year

The Fifth Season

By Barbara Kunz Loots

♛ Hallmark Editions

PHOTO CREDITS
Richard Brown: *Page 45.*
Ed Cooper: *Cover.*
Van Cleve Photography: *Page 4.*
Dick Fanolio: *Pages 20, 33.*
Fred Kautt: *Page 40.*
Joe Klemovich: *Title Page, Pages 9, 16.*
Bob Kurt: *Page 25.*
Rick Lyons: *Page 13.*
Bob Segura: *Page 28.*
Gary West: *Page 36.*

Designed by Rick Lyons.

Outside my kitchen window, the maples are turning again to gold and wine and rust, and I can hear the shouts and laughter of children on their way to school. Suddenly I become one of them, remembering the swish and crunch of leaves underfoot, feeling the excitement of first school days again. And the present autumn dissolves into a fifth season — the season of my heart.

Each of the four seasons turns my thoughts to something new. With every change, nature reveals fresh insight into living and being myself. It is the same for you — in your own season of the heart. For in this "fifth season," you and I see landscapes comprised of a thousand pictures from our memories and our dreams. The weather changes from sun to shadow according to our feelings and moods. Yet, while the years go by from winter to spring and summer to fall, time stands still. And we realize that it is always now in the season of the heart.

Though silent and cold on the surface, winter for me is a season for nurturing and for beginnings. Now, all life finds shelter, strengthens its roots and gathers its resources to emerge at some later time reborn—perhaps better than before.

City dwellers seldom are snowbound. Yet winter still has an effect of isolation. Into my corner, without excuse to the sun and the sky, I can retreat to relish my memories and to renew my dreams.

Fire flickers on the hearth. Content in its presence, I study it. No two fires are alike in the way their flames dance and colors flash, and yet the result is always warmth and light. Fires are like friends.

Perhaps even more than the bare-skin days of summer, winter sharpens my senses. I become more aware of color because it is rare. I become more aware of my body because of the weight and texture of clothing and the tingle of freezing air on my ears. And the cold wind I breathe in and exhale again in a warm cloud of breath makes me remember the delicate life within.

The full moon on luminous snow makes a moonscape of earth. And we are the moonpeople leaving our curious tracks through the space of night.

I know a wilderness farther away than the moon and more mysterious than the sea. It is the unexplored space in me, and I am continually traveling. This journey takes every moment of time I have. And _now_ is wherever I happen to be.

Last night an ice storm created a terrible beauty, a crystalline wreckage of trees. Shattered limbs lie everywhere. Some trees are nearly split in two. Yet, there are many branches bent down to the ground with the weight of the ice, and they are not broken. They will revive. How often have I remained stiff and proud when bending instead would bring life?

Despite the feeling of confinement, winter generates its own kind of energy in me. Perhaps winter days seem too short to let important tasks remain undone. And the electric current created by my activity helps to make amends for the missing sun.

There is an expectant feeling late in the winter. Life slows down a little. Unfinished projects lose importance and old plans give way to new—the contemplation of garden catalogs picturing dreams in delicious flavors and promises already in bloom.

Suddenly, ahead of schedule, spring arrives for a single day. Open the windows! Open the doors! Let in clean light and laundered air. Let loose the dust clouds that settled in over the winter and bring out the bright, fresh upholstery of flowers and daydreams and neighborliness!

Spring shows a beautiful face. But for me it is a season of contrasts, when both my sorrows and joys seem the keenest and most confused. For example, there is my lawn. How I hate the burgeoning weeds that must be pulled out! And yet, how I love them, because they are dandelions, filling my yard with their bright little buttons of sun!

I try to pay attention now—to see, to hear, to touch the tiny miracles that are occurring. There are barely visible knots, not quite buds yet, on the branches, that create a reddish tint in the treetops. Almost as I watch, the buds swell and baby leaves burst through, flashing a green signal—Go! Spring!

Now the "new" year really arrives, without the burden of resolutions. Now I am free. There is no hurry. It is the youth of the year and most of it still lies ahead.

The jonquils always catch me by surprise. Their long fingers feel upward through the earth and grass beside the bushes long before I look for them. Spring comes, whether I am watching or not. I'm glad!

I used to fall in love so predictably every spring I began to mistrust the emotion. Then I fell really in love and discovered a springtime that never ends.

Some birds are building a nest in the tree by the porch. It is woven with bits of my yarn which had strayed outdoors, with packing material tossed from a gift sent by a faraway friend, even with strands of my hair, I think. It makes me wonder how carefully I conserve, how creatively I use, the scraps of time, the bits of talent, the small opportunities that are mine. I must keep that nest, like a little scrapbook of nature, for a reminder after the birds have flown.

An awesome rush of swirling clouds sends me to the windows to watch like a ship's captain, as though my house might sink in the storm. The sky looks like a silver and black kaleidoscope of clouds as I post my lookout for the whirling fist of the wind.

Green has a fragrance, almost a taste, like the essence of grass, blended in morning mist, laced with the sheer zest of being alive! Green smells wet, pure, zing-y, joyful, promising. Green smells…green.

Summer is as full of sound as spring is full of fragrance. Raucous birds and barking dogs, music broadcast on the wind and the sound of laughter as life moves outdoors. I listen to the vehicles and voices of people playing and building and roaming about in the noisy freedom of summer, and feel like a member of one big family again.

I like to watch the heat create shimmering pools of unreal water where the street curves over a rise. A mirage is but a reflection of faraway things--a wavering vision that disappears the closer it comes, like the future itself. Perhaps if I spent fewer moments admiring mirages I might discover more beautiful, real things right at my feet that would not disappear.

A mountain of clouds cracks in two, and the torrent comes like an avalanche with a darkness quicker than night. Then, suddenly, sun bursts through again, and all the leaves drop diamonds. In that still, beautiful moment, nothing breathes in wonder.

One summer when I was a child, we lived by a sound—a stem of ocean between two shores. There, on the barren beach, I realized trees do not make the wind move, but the other way around. Next time the wind blows, I think I shall try to imagine the trees are whipping the air into breezes. Sometimes I think my child eyes saw things best.

Summer is time suspended in the thick air of afternoons. I can condition the air, but I cannot alter that summertime feeling that for any task, tomorrow is soon enough.

There are three especially magnificent moments
unique to a summer day, when the universe seems to
focus on where I stand...

...first, the earliest light of the long summer morning
when damp air deliciously shivers the spine--one of
the few times nearest to silence left to a noisy world...

...second, the lingering twilight, when stars fall into
meteors--fall, perhaps, into fireflies! Even the crickets
are like little stars, a galaxy of sound in the grass...

...third of these wonderful moments--discovering each plump, ripe tomato that hangs on the stem like fulfillment itself. When I pick them, I feel like a sister to all generations of earth...and I am the one who is born in the summer of Time.

Usually, autumn arrives unexpectedly, tosses a lace curtain of frost over the windows, and moves in to stay awhile. After the initial shock, she is an invigorating guest!

The wind-strewn fragments of falling leaves contradict, in a sense, the spirit of autumn. To me, now is a time, not of scattering, but of gathering. Everywhere, people are coming together again from the independence of summer. I go back with them into various places where all of us gathered before...to learn and to teach, to work and to worship, to start in, refreshed, at a faster pace.

Fall is a time of excitement shaped by our early years. In my mind, I put on new shoes and sharpen my pencils and wait for the bus of adventure to pick me up!

As I watch the flights of birds filling the autumn sky,
I wish I knew their names and where they have been
and where they are going. They and the squirrels and
the little rabbit who stole from my garden all summer
and all other earthbound creatures anticipate winter
together. As I stack the wood and secure the windows,
I feel a natural kinship even with these wild things.

The nights turn cold and the house begins to creak.
Even the ghosts are moving back indoors.

Sometimes we know people only in context. That is, we are with them at work, for example, or only on social occasions. Visiting such a friend at her home for the first time, I noticed her garden where zinnias and marigolds bloomed in a brilliant autumn revival. They were, however, almost overwhelmed by weeds and grass gone wild. I was astonished by this disorder. "That is not like you," I said. She smiled for a silent moment. Then I realized people, including myself, have many more worlds than the one any two of us share.

The green of summer drains from the leaves, revealing their beautiful inner colors--yellow and amber and red. As I leave behind another cycle of seasons, I wonder--have my inner colors begun to show?

The trees are leafless now, except for the stubborn pin oak. Its leaves cling to the branches like little brown hands refusing to let go of summer. Who will remind them spring lies ahead?

In autumn, I sense a ripeness and readiness in myself. I have loved the fragrant and colorful bloom. I have danced in the shade of the cool green branches...

...and now, as I savor the fruit and the flavor of living in whatever moments have fallen to me, I realize that my seedbed of memories and my harvest of dreams are still part of me...

...and I know that the most important moment in time, whatever the season, whether of dreams or of doing, of planting or gathering, fragrance or fruit...the only moment in time that matters is Now. Always.